THE WAY OF KNOWLEDGE

THE WAY OF KNOWLEDGE

MANAGING THE UNMANAGEABLE

Stowe Boyd

Writers Club Press
San Jose New York Lincoln Shanghai

The Way of Knowledge
Managing the Unmanageable

Writers Club Press
an imprint of iUniverse.com, Inc.

For information address:
iUniverse.com, Inc.
5220 S 16th, Ste. 200
Lincoln, NE 68512
www.iuniverse.com

ISBN: 0-595-15046-2

Printed in the United States of America

Contents

Foreword

This book presents a number of the apparent contra-
dictions that surround the issues of leadership in
knowledge-driven business. The central metaphor of
the book is the Zen koan—a juxtaposition of opposing
or apparently contradictory concepts for the purpose
of inducing insight in the listener—but I must confess
that I am no Buddhist adept, and I profess no towering
spiritual enlightenment. If anything, I could be considered a mundane business philosopher, and a very secu-
lar one at that.

This notwithstanding, I have come to appreciate
(through my admittedly superficial exploration of
Buddhism) the concept of the "sudden school" in Zen
doctrine, where enlightenment can be attained in a
moment, given the right circumstances, the right words,

the right mindset. It is in this spirit that I offer *The Way of Knowledge.*

In a way, this book snuck up on me, and I am almost surprised that it has come into being. It is the logical conclusion to thoughts I have presented in my writing and lectures over the past few years.

I am wholly responsible for the inadequacies of this work. Those who have sponsored, guided, inspired, and tolerated me, whether they know it or not, are largely responsible for anything of value you may find here.

The list is too long to note here, but these are a few of the most deserving of recognition: McLuhan, Senge, Bateson, Wiener, Fuller, Drucker, Handy, Kauffman, and Porter, for setting the context; all my teachers, even the ones I didn't listen to; business partners, past, present, and future, for showing me how to hold on and when to let go; to Martha and Tom, for starting me out; and to Sarah, Keenan, and Conrad, for everything else.

Knowledge and Learning

In times of discontinuous change, established paradigms fail. We are in such a time, when our thinking about learning and knowledge in business is undergoing a dramatic, and necessary, revolution.

Perhaps this should come as no surprise. Spinning at the center of all innovation is learning and the application of knowledge. We have come to appreciate the key role of innovation in business. The barrage of popular business books extolling flexibility and agility simply use physical, sports-oriented metaphors to describe accelerated learning. What, after all, is "corporate agility" other than learning to learn faster? Arie de Geus was certainly too tentative when he said, "Perhaps the only sustainable competitive advantage is the capacity to learn."

As the world speeds up, we have become increasingly aware that we need to adopt a new attitude about learning and knowledge in business, and to move it to center stage.

We know intellectually that the value of a business is increasingly driven by intangibles, such as the knowledge in people's heads. But we continue on, managing and tracking business based on tangibles-based accounting, with knowledge assets not shown on the balance sheet.

We need to develop a second, perhaps imaginary, set of books; not with the goal of beating the tax system, but with the goal of deprogramming ourselves, of breaking with the cult of industrial thinking and moving learning and knowledge to their rightful and pivotal position in our corporate and personal agendas.

We are reluctant to consider learning central, but why? Perhaps we sense that we are not investing enough, personally and in the enterprise, in learning.

Business success and strategy has long been cast in such swashbuckling terms—"the art of war" and so on—that the thought of a modern enterprise organized along the lines of a summer camp, a quilting bee, or a jazz ensemble is perhaps unsettling to business leaders, confronted as they are with the need to redefine the concept of leadership itself in this new and turbulent era.

This book is subtitled "Managing the Unmanageable" —which is not intended to suggest that leadership is impossible today—but rather to force re-evaluation of the basic premises of management in the knowledge-driven company.

While not exactly an oxymoron, knowledge management is a slippery concept. Why? Because knowledge is personal. It is a set of related logical postulates and experiences in the mind of an individual, not a physical asset, like manufacturing equipment.

How can we manage that which resides within the minds of others, intangible, invisible, unknowable? How can we manage the unmanageable?

Alas, in this book I offer no great 12-step plan to answering this question, but instead offer a number of questions that, I hope, shed light on various aspects of the issue. Of course, you have the harder job of finding some resolution of the issues, on your own terms, in your own time.

I have chosen the easier job by far.

The Leader as Beginner

Leadership seems an obvious word. In the world of business, leadership has taken on a multiplicity of meanings, ranging from fascism to the mystical. While some of what is said about leadership may inspire us, many business people are confused about the nature of leadership today. We are in a time of unprecedented change, and today's futurists tell us that the rate of change in technology, in commerce, and in our markets is accelerating. We are not headed for a millennial plateau, where the amazing advances of the last fifty years can be slowly evaluated, analyzed, and selectively assimilated. On the contrary, we are headed for exponential change in the next decade.

As an example, consider the number of recent technological innovations with which you come into contact every day: ATMs, PDAs, car-sensing traffic signals, cellular phones, air bags, digital signatures, PCs, laser scanners, and so on. At the end of the next ten years, you can expect to have ten times as many innovations in everyday use. These are things which are today unnamed, and perhaps, unimagined, but which will emerge and move into common use, as did microwaves and pagers in the last decade.

This is the world before us. It is not simply a world of rampant expansion of consumer goods, but of nearly unchecked innovation in every business domain. This is the new context for leadership, today and tomorrow. While many other forces drive or hinder effective leadership, the one feature of our times that will dominate the agenda of business leaders is accommodating increasingly accelerated change.

For every process, technique, technology, and channel in use today imagine ten or more arising or replacing earlier alternatives in the next ten years. Imagine new competitors, new forms of employment, an accelerated financial and regulatory environment, you name it. Success in business will come from driving and accommodating change, of understanding and adapting to new challenges, new realities, and new opportunities, and doing so more quickly than others.

This is learning, plain and simple. Or, perhaps, not so simple. The rate of change has increased beyond the point where our ways of learning can keep up. We have to rethink the management of business, reworking work itself to build learning in.

The value chain—the means of delivering value to clients—has become the navel of managerial contemplation. Our obsession with value for the customer is laudable, and has led to a redistribution of the surplus value derived from industrial efficiency.

Now, we will have to balance the value chain with the knowledge chain, where we build enough time to learn, and to capture and share what we know into our business processes, strategies, organization, and personal lives. We have to rebuild the boat while sailing in higher winds, never having time to put it in dry dock.

So the business leader needs to be a perpetual beginner, constantly learning, constantly trying new things, constantly building better systems to balance the knowledge chain and the value chain.

Always beginning, never done.

Familiar Paradoxes of Leadership and Knowledge

0. The Way of Knowledge

Our transition into the knowledge economy will not be smooth, but a time of chaotic change. Today's economy is not an extrapolation of yesterday's economy, and is not just more of the same stuff speeded-up. We are moving through a phase shift, where some of the critical factors of the previous era are now irrelevant, and others have now moved into prominence. We are going through a revolution.

To be brutally honest, human psychology is basically unprepared for radical change. *Homo Sapiens* evolved over millions of years in which tomorrow was nearly indistinguishable from yesterday. As innovation has gained momentum in the past few hundred years since the Renaissance and through the Industrial Age, we developed, at no small cost, a new perception of the world and our place in it.

Now again we are confronted with the driving need to rethink the basic principles that motivate our work and business, and how to thrive and grow in a new context. We need to examine the new realities:

- The value of a business is no longer principally based on tangible assets, such as railroad cars or flourmills, but on intangibles, such as mind-share and manufacturing adaptability.
- Information technology is the prime mover of the new economy, and those who master IT increase their chances of success in existing markets, and ease their entry in other markets.
- Our ways of management are largely leftovers from the industrial era of the immediate past, and are not naturally workable in this new context.

I have mentioned that the leader must be a beginner. Where do we begin our lessons? Every business leader should start by evaluating the company's knowledge chain: the patterns and programs that support knowledge sharing, the policies governing education and the application of learning, reward systems that do or don't acknowledge learning and knowledge, and perhaps most importantly, the balance between the value chain and the knowledge chain.

A company's knowledge chain often operates fortuitously, where we first hire well-educated people, provide them with a minimal amount of on-going learning, and rely on the natural transfer of knowledge as people bump into each other in the course of events. This worked well when the number of workers was relatively small; they encountered each other frequently; they developed on-going relationships; and they had many opportunities to learn from each other. In the knowledge economy, people still bump into each other, but the velocity is so fast, the duration of the bump is so short, and the number of different people we bump is so high, that this approach fails to foster knowledge transfer.

The leader must balance apparently opposing interests: the value chain (which delivers value to customers and makes money for the business) and the knowledge chain (which transfers knowledge from person to person, increases the value of individuals, and indirectly increases the value and vitality of the company).

The way of knowledge is accepting the necessary tension between short-term, transitory value delivery and the long-term, enduring knowledge development, and then working to find and keep a balance between them.

1. The Way of Authority

Those who would have the greatest influence must cede authority

The complex dynamic between leading and controlling is central in knowledge management, where the assets are personal and intangible, and much of the value of "followership" in the organization is invisible.

Consider the various parts of the knowledge cycle, and how many ways management control, when imperfectly applied, can hinder it. Knowledge exists in the mind of an individual as a personal asset. To transfer the knowledge, the knower must capture the knowledge in a shared language—either natural language, or a formal language, like mathematics, architectural drawings, or business process models—to externalize the knowledge as an impersonal asset. Note that this asset is not the knowledge, but a model of it; an artifact intended to help others learn and gain insight.

If others become involved in a learning-based collaboration with the knower, then other information that provides interpersonal support for the knowledge transfer may be added to the model. If someone internalizes the model, makes the knowledge personal, and gains understanding, then the knowledge cycle is complete.

In this learning cycle there are a variety of possible transitions as knowledge moves from personal to impersonal, from impersonal to interpersonal, from interpersonal to personal. Often some of these transitions may be skipped. For example, culinary knowledge moves from personal to interpersonal, and inter-personal to personal, without any external models when a student works closely with a master chef. Likewise, learning can take place without interpersonal intermediates through reading.

The leader plays no direct role in the knowledge cycle, unless as a knower or learner. A leader who tries to force decisions, to coerce the activities in the cycle or the direction they take, will simply degrade the cycle. Leaders cannot command insight, demand collaboration, or control thought. The rise of the concept of "anti-heroic management" in the past few years is an outcome of the positive effects of leaders relaxing the principle of control.

Control of the knowledge cycle—to the degree that it is controlled at all—lies in the hands of the participants. Like the Heisenberg uncertainty principle, we find that the insertion of managerial authority slows or breaks the knowledge cycle.

Leaders must reject the concept of authoritarian management, and work through indirect influence, by rethinking policies, incentives, and investment strategy. Only by ceding authority over knowledge transfer can leaders influence others to learn and share knowledge.

2. The Way of Ownership

Those who would be valued by their knowledge must cede ownership

Knowledge is personal and is, therefore, possessed by individuals. While legal ownership of processes, patents, and intellectual property may reside within the control of the enterprise, people are the medium for knowledge application.

Individuals possess their knowledge, and are valued because of the enterprise's critical need for that knowledge and their understanding of how to apply it. It seems natural that knowledge and its application could be considered a critical resource, and increasing its scarcity by hoarding would increase the value of the knower. However, personal knowledge is valued most highly when it is transferred to others, thereby decreasing the relative scarcity of knowledge.

In supply-and-demand economics, this wouldn't make sense: giving away diamonds would drive down the price, and hoarding would drive up the price diamonds. This is an economic mechanism that is well understood by the diamond cartels.

The economics of knowledge is like the economics of a network, in which value increases with the number of users. Paradoxically, the knowledge worker is more valuable the more that he gives away his most precious resource. By giving up the concept of personal ownership of knowledge, and by enlisting others to jointly "own" knowledge critical to the success of the business, the knowledge worker increases his or her value to the enterprise.

A famous example of knowledge hoarding is Newton's concealment of his invention of calculus. Rather than share his innovation, he presented his proofs in algebraic and geometric forms for decades. It wasn't until Leibnitz independently discovered and published his version of calculus (we use his symbology today) that Newton shared his personal version. It is obvious today that Leibnitz's act increased the value of Newton's work exponentially. Newton might have gone to his grave never sharing his breakthrough. While we would perhaps still honor his memory as a scholar, he may not have played as pivotal a role in the realm of modern physics…and world civilization would have been worse off for it.

In business, we have Newtons in every division who are hoarding some key technique or tool, and getting personal reward and status for it. We can't rely on a Leibnitz to show up, so we need to convince everyone that knowledge kept hidden is knowledge held back. Leaders must encourage and reward for knowledge networking, and rework the culture and business policies wherever they find knowledge hoarding.

3. The Way of Commerce

The core axis of the commercial relationship is not commerce, but the search for knowledge

The movement into a new economy is not superficial; it is not just the old order speeded up. It has inverted one of the most basic psychological and cultural beliefs: the fundamental dynamic of the commercial relationship is the exchange of money for goods.

It seems intuitive that the linkage between the consumer and the vendor of a product is principally oriented around the product, its purchase and delivery. This is a superficial approximation of the actual dynamics of the relationship.

Sadly, we have internalized the premises of mass marketing to such a great extent that we find it hard to push our thinking out of the deep ruts left behind by our enculturation through mass media. We have come to think of the map as the territory.

Where is the error? First, the customer is not a nameless, faceless member of a market segment. He or she is a specific individual, involved in moving forward in the knowledge economy. The customer's interest in a product or service is part of larger issues that are not strictly tied to price or product features.

From this perspective, the vendor is primarily in the business of assisting others to meet the challenges of the environment. Likewise, by selecting our product or services, the client is helping us to meet the challenges of the marketplace. Here, the primary medium of exchange is not money, but information.

I formalize this observation into the following law of new commercial value: The compounded value of the information that could be exchanged in any transaction is greater than the current economic value of the transaction itself. The money changing hands is like the two friends taking turns buying lunch. The momentary exchange of money is nearly incidental to the long-term value of the relationship.

Note that the long-term value of the information being exchanged is largely intangible, and that value can only be realized downstream if the vendor can capture and apply the available information. If we lived in a "frictionless" environment, where no information was lost, and all information was translated into applicable knowledge, the tangible exchange of value would be unnecessary. Information itself would serve as currency.

The second flaw of our unthinking approach to commerce is the view that the sole purpose of the business is to make money. Admittedly, businesses exist to turn a profit, create value, and provide a livelihood for its employees. But, in the knowledge economy, the underlying dynamic that makes all of those things possible is the transfer of knowledge. The tie between parties to a commercial relationship is learning—the enterprise needs to learn about the individual's reasons for buying (or not buying) the product, and customers are learning to advance their interests.

A company that is delivering critical knowledge embedded in products and services will not lack money.

4. The Way of Education

Business education must serve the firm, but learning is personal and selfish

Today's training programs, where corporate planners attempt to anticipate what workers need to know are something like the five-year plans of the now defunct Soviet Bloc, and they fail for the same reasons: The world is changing too fast for a single, central staff group to adequately anticipate what individuals will need to know.

There is no effective halfway solution. The only alternative is to accept that individuals need to develop their own personal learning plans, which must be subsidized by the firm, even when the utility of the learning program is not immediately obvious.

This means that if Janet in accounting wants to study foreign languages, not contract law, the company leadership should roll with it, not veto it. Who can be certain that Janet will benefit the firm more by learning the Uniform Commercial Code instead of Portuguese?

Only individuals acting on their own personal agendas and advancing their own selfish ends can accelerate the company's knowledge. Attempting to restrictively channel people's learning along preordained lines will not only fail (since people will not learn unless they actively are interested) but has the possibility of failing catastrophically.

We know from ecology that the animals best adapted to circumscribed environmental niches are the first to die off in the face of ecological change, while the more flexible generalists live on. Ecologists refer to this diversity of behaviors and physical traits within a population of animals that allows them to adapt to a wide range of environmental conditions as "requisite variety." Note that there is no "invisible hand" making these genetic choices. It is the emergent result of the uncountable independent actions and decisions of all the individuals in the population.

Knowledge is the DNA of business. As in the natural world, where strict control of genetic interaction can quickly lead to a decrease in requisite variety, in business, controlling knowledge interactions limits the creation and sharing of knowledge, and deters innovation.

In times of environmental stability, maximum adaptation to a single niche is a good strategy, which genes and business have exploited from time immemorial. However, in times of great change, occupying and dominating a single ecological niche is a dangerous game. Rather than behaving like the panda, that lives only in bamboo groves and eats only one sort of leaf, our businesses would do better to emulate the raccoon, which can live anywhere and eat nearly anything.

The knowledge assets of the firm emerge from the stewpot of many individuals learning what they think is important for themselves. Their consideration of the enterprise's agenda is only secondary. The more leaders go with this natural tendency, the faster they increase the variety and diversity of thinking in the firm, and gain the adaptability and flexibility needed to thrive today and beyond.

5. The Way of Economics

While intangible, the economics of knowledge are more fundamental than tangible economics

It is an interesting historical footnote that modern bookkeeping was invented during the Renaissance. The explosion in economic activity at that time led, of necessity, to the formulation of cost accounting, and the association of tangible costs with tangible returns.

In an era when value is increasingly based on intangibles, we should not manage our companies on cost accounting alone. Managing costs is like taking vitamins. They don't directly provide good health—for that, good diet and regular exercise are much more critical—but they won't hurt you either. By all means, manage costs; take vitamins.

Most companies' economic thinking is firmly grounded in costs, not value. The stock market valuation of firms is based largely on the assessment of intangibles, like perception of value, anticipated market growth, and economic position, as well as the company's balance sheet.

Since the intangibles are not on the balance sheet, we must work like a shady accountant who keeps a second set of books. However, we are not seeking to conceal income from the taxman, or launder illegal cash—we are trying to more accurately understand the return on investments made in knowledge-related activities, which often yield intangibles long before tangible results flow.

You might ask yourself these questions, or use them to initiate a dialogue with your partners regarding knowledge economics and knowledge accounting:
- What are our knowledge assets?
- What system is used to value these assets?
- How are knowledge assets being invested in the creation and accumulation of new knowledge?

Think about new economic activities that should be integrated into your firm:
- What is our return on knowledge investments?
- Should I undertake a knowledge audit? How?
- How can we reward those most active in the development and application of valuable intangible assets?

We may need a new bookkeeping discipline to adequately understand and guide the economic life of knowledge-driven companies. The first step is to simply realize that the real value of a business is like the value of a book. You can't assess a book's value by its number of pages, its weight, or even its price.

This argument for knowledge economics does not mean we must retreat to esthetics in our assessment of value, but simply to ratify our appreciation of the utility of knowledge, and begin to measure it.

6. The Way of Participation

Everyone is a knowledge worker, even if they (or you) don't believe it

Recently, I was invited to attend a knowledge management summit, sponsored by a well-known industry publication. In one session, the issue of involvement in knowledge programs was raised and pushed around by the attendees.

The president of a software firm suggested that, based on his experience, not all people could (or should) participate in learning or the sharing of knowledge. I am sure that the policies in his firm bear out this observation, with those "lower" in the organization demonstrating their lack of "big picture" orientation and a reliance on "higher-ups" to make the key decisions. I strenuously disagreed with my colleague's stance, and made the comment that in the knowledge economy, everyone is a knowledge worker. His view to the contrary is a dangerous, self-fulfilling prophecy.

Why is it dangerous? Those viewed as incapable of acting as knowledge workers will be excluded from opportunities to develop, formalize, and share their knowledge. Their lack of involvement with the knowledge activities going on around them will reinforce the official wisdom that they have nothing valuable to contribute to the company's knowledge assets or processes. I am reminded of Frederick Douglas' comment about slave owners who complained about the dirtiness of field hands, without ever giving them time or materials to wash.

This view is a manifestation of the concept of knowledge as a scarce resource, which as such, needs to be administered by the managerial class. However, knowledge is not a pile of diamonds to be hoarded, but a network to be shared, the value of which increases with the number of connections.

The greatest knowledge acceleration occurs when every person is viewed as a knowledge worker, linked to the knowledge network, and whose greatest contributions will come from the application of intellect to business performance. The contributor's job title and seniority do not matter. Important contributions may come from the newest hire on the marketing team, the chief knowledge officer, or the receptionist.

A lifetime of counter-examples may have led you to believe that you (or others) are just performing tasks determined by others. If so, you are squandering talent. It is a universal fact of human psychology that everyone (unless mentally ill) wants to know more, do better, help others, and succeed, even when circumstances have conspired to convince them otherwise.

Reversing cultural patterns can be hard; especially when certain kinds of workers—like clerical staff or field sales reps—are viewed as wind-up automata that have little impact on the value delivered by the firm. A wholesale shift in thinking about participation in the knowledge economy is needed.

Think network, not diamonds.

7. The Way of Emergence

Knowledge sharing is natural, so we need to artificially recreate natural workplaces

The behavior (and success) of a company emerges from the interplay of individuals, and not from management edict. So it is essential to create an environment where natural interplay is encouraged, and where the unnaturalness of modern, hectic business life is countered with tools, methods, and cultural norms that support knowledge acceleration. For example, in large firms, individuals may travel a great deal, and work in teams with different people on short-term assignments. This leads to decreased face-time, less group interplay, and fewer opportunities to transfer knowledge.

Companies need to counter these forces with company-wide information technologies that support knowledge transfer, programs that reward the application of impersonal knowledge assets, and explicit mentoring of younger workers by older, more experienced (and presumably more knowledgeable) senior workers.

This may seem only reasonable, but it is common that these practices are either not undertaken at all, or treated as just one more distraction from the "real" activities of the business, like selling or production. To be considered "real" work, we need to reward involvement in structured knowledge transfer programs, and to carve out time to participate in them.

Many people labor under intense time pressures and believe that personal heroism—working long hours, being constantly available, and sacrificing personal interests—are a requirement for success. To the extent that your business is inculcating this dogma, it is failing not only the individuals involved but also the long-term viability of the company.

This is analogous to speeding up the assembly line in a factory—burning people out and eliminating any time for reflection and interaction, or personal learning. In effect this approach squeezes out knowledge and learning activities, without which doing business becomes mere drudgery.

What is natural? The natural pattern of knowledge transfer can be thought of as a cycle. It starts with an individual capturing some knowledge in a sharable, impersonal form, like a blueprint, document, story, or diagram. Others are exposed to the impersonal knowledge asset, either in solitary or interpersonal interpretation of the knowledge artifact. For many people, this interpersonal interpretation is the fastest and most productive way to learn. Finally, the knowledge is recreated through learning and insight in the heads of individuals.

Much of the attractiveness of groupware and intranets is nothing more than breaking the time-and-space barrier that the modern business has erected between people, a barrier that degrades the rate of learning and the rich interchange of ideas that people thrive on in close collaborative groups.

I expect a new generation of "know-ware" products to emerge, which elaborate on the communication paradigm of groupware, and explicitly focus on learning and knowledge sharing.

8. The Way of Trust

First trust, then trustworthiness

Much of what I have offered as guidance to leaders involves rethinking the job of leading. There is perhaps no more difficult a reappraisal than that of trust. A leader cannot compel others to do the right thing, but can only inspire others to do something, and to trust them to do the right thing according to their own logic.

Often what others choose to do is not exactly what we would have done, given the circumstances. But measuring against "what I might have done" is often the least helpful metric to hold up. Just consider the extreme extension of this policy: if everyone did things just like you, the company would be full of clones.

The gift of diversity comes wrapped in the paper of conflict and the ribbon of confusion. We have to deal with the wrapping to get to the gift.

An important aspect of every business opportunity is the chance to learn, so the first metric should be how much has been learned. In fact, no so-called "failure" is a failure unless we fail to learn from it. One task for the leader is to challenge others to expand their horizons, test their talents and skills, and confront them with opportunities to learn and make choices. Leaders have to trust people to make the best choice according to their own lights.

If we have concerns as leaders about the abilities of our colleagues to make good decisions, we are in fact criticizing our learning programs (or lack of programs). A situation where people appear to be unprepared to make good decisions is really a cue that something important is missing.

The common alternative—sequestering decision making within an elite managerial group—is simply wrong. Why? Elitism fails in two ways. First, elitism fails to take advantage of the massive parallelism of the company's total intelligence, and unnaturally blocks those closest to problems from resolving them. Second, elitism disincents the non-elite from taking responsibility outside of their pigeonhole, which leads to alienation, diminished value delivery to the customer, and slower learning.

Trusting everyone is a revolutionary act. Trust extends beyond the realm of personal learning and pervades everything in the company. Carried to its logical conclusion, we have to trust people to choose the work they should do, to choose who they want to work with, and how to deliver value to the client.

We need to balance freedom with responsibility, or else we have mere license. However, all the support in the world for the cycles of learning and knowledge will prove to be superfluous unless those doing the learning can ultimately choose how to apply the knowledge they have gained.

9. The Way of Language

Abstractions are the basis of knowledge practice

One definition of business knowledge is the understanding of the interrelationships between critical factors that influence the success of the business.

Capturing a personal awareness of the context, content, and concept of some domain of knowledge in an impersonal language, or model, requires abstraction. To distill the salient and drop out the non-essential, to highlight interrelationships and ignore the incidental, to find the general in the specific and the timeless in the moment—this is the value of abstraction.

We need richer languages in which to capture our understanding about the inter-relatedness of critical factors. We need to move beyond a reliance on natural languages (like English and Swahili) as the sole means of communicating about business. Natural language is linear. We make one statement, followed by another, and then perhaps make an assertion about the relationship between the first statement and the second. "If such-and-such holds," we say, "Then so-and-so will happen."

The problem is that many of the most central business issues are not linear, but cyclic. Cause-and-effect thinking is really too limited and bounded to capture the inter-dependencies in business. The most practical application of learning and knowledge requires abstract languages. This may seem counter-intuitive, but abstract languages—such as systems dynamics, object inheritance, game theory, and complexity theory—can create a context for thinking and discussion which is not possible with natural languages.

I refer to this as the "Way of Language," since learning how to think abstractly and how to apply the insights that abstract thinking offers can involve the longest and shallowest learning curve of all the practices discussed in *The Way of Knowledge*.

The knowledge transfer cycle pivots on the availability of abstract languages, in which personal knowledge can be abstracted and captured in an impersonal form, like a musical score, a cookie recipe, or a mathematical formula. Others who know the language of music, cooking, or mathematics can read what has been captured and understand what is intended. Interpersonal group activities—like a jazz quartet trying out a new piece or a mathematics colloquium puzzling over some new equations—can often be the fastest path to knowledge transfer, much faster than individual, solitary learning.

Once captured, knowledge assets can continue to influence decisions, stimulate learning, and facilitate collaboration long after having been written down. It has been said that one cannot have an idea that is inexpressible in one's native language. By learning new languages leaders enable themselves and their colleagues to think new thoughts.

For these new times, leaders need to create and adopt new knowledge-oriented business languages.

10. The Way of Leadership

Knowledge can't be managed, but that is the leader's job

Leadership in the knowledge era is a paradox, a seeming contradiction that each leader must confront and work through. We know that knowledge is the outcome, almost a side effect, of the workings of the human mind, a region well outside the direct control of managers. At a superficial level, if managers try to coercively control knowledge, their labors amount to nothing. Myopic programs to catalog and organize knowledge as if it were dry goods in a warehouse—while leading to a better appreciation of the value of knowledge—fundamentally miss the point. They never move into the realm of personalized understanding, where the potential value of knowledge is articulated into business results.

The company is not a machine, even though we have described it in mechanical metaphors for so many generations that we have internalized the metaphor as reality. Gregory Bateson offered the observation that "The only productive way to think of a business is as a network of conversations." In reality the company is a society of people, brought together by common purposes: a village, a neighborhood, a super-organism, and not a machine at all.

Moving past the superficial, leaders have to rethink control as an aspect of management, and give up the obsession of control; especially since the object of management interest has shifted from materiel to thought. Picasso once said that the artist must start each new creation by breaking his brushes. He meant rethinking the practice of his art. Similarly, those that would manage the business must enter the new economy by rethinking the concepts of management, and employing a new set of skills to accomplish new aims.

Accepting the apparently paradoxical task of managing the unmanageable is a powerful dynamic that can drive the interests of the company forward. To do so, management practices must rely on indirection, on the emergent behavior of individuals seeking their own paths, and on the balanced values of trust, responsibility, and self-interest.

I have sometimes called this "managerial jiu-jitsu," since the image of a 90-pound adept using the kinetic energy of a 200-pound antagonist to counter the attacking force is inspiring. At the same time the martial context can be misleading, and should be balanced with more benign and peaceful images. I view the role of the leader more like that of gardener or parent. Kahlil Gibran wrote that "Children are arrows we shoot into the future." an image that suggests the role of management in the new world. Managers influence individuals who make up the company, and the future is then firmly in the individuals' hands, hearts, and, more cogently, in their minds.

Leadership now means accepting the paradox of managing the unmanageable: acknowledging the impossibility of a static balance between the knowledge imperatives for the business, which applies the knowledge assets, and those of the individuals, who are the real owners of knowledge. The leader's challenge is to find and maintain balance, while accelerating business momentum.

Like the gardener who knows that the plants do all the work of growing even though the gardener provides the tending and watering, company leaders should know that by providing a learning environment and letting the workers do the work of learning, the knowledge of the company will grow.

Ideas and Change

There is a cybernetic theory that asserts that ideas, like viruses, have a life of their own, apart from us, but only realized through us. In this school of thought, ideas, when considered independently of those holding them, are called *memes*, and we are their hosts.

Samuel Butler once remarked, "A chicken is an egg's means to create more eggs." In this light, our minds are the medium that ideas create to propagate themselves, and the outcome is that we infect each other with new ideas, which spread exactly like diseases, from one person to another.

My intention here is not to distance myself from authorship: this is my work, and I stand by it. At the same time, my thinking is the outgrowth of other's whose ideas have changed me, I think, for the better. So, at a deeper level, this book is openly subversive. I am open about my aim: to make the world a better place to live and work.

I hope the ideas here are no longer mine, that they have spun out of my control, and are, to some extent, changing you and your thinking about the world. I approach this opportunity to plant some memes on you, like some crazed bio-terrorist in a science fiction novel, hoping that you will become infected with these ideas and spread them.

I hope you will carry away at least a few of these ideas, these memes, like seedlings or cuttings gathered on a trip to the woods. I hope that you will plant them or graft them in your own environment, in your business or college or government agency. I hope that they will thrive, and others, your colleagues, partners and clients, will come to do the same through interaction with you and the memes that you carry.

Embracing the central role of knowledge and learning in business and society forces us to rework everything. It is a revolutionary insight, just as the concept of unalienable rights transformed the political and moral landscape; as Kepler's, Newton's, and Einstein's physics shifted our perception of the cosmos time and time again; and as Darwin's evolutionary theory forced a re-evaluation of *Homo Sapiens'* place in the universe.

Once an insight is lodged within the mind, the clock cannot be turned back, the transformation cannot be undone, Humpty-Dumpty cannot be put back together again.

We are all agents of change, since we are the medium through which all change occurs. There is no nameless, faceless "they" making this change, there is no disembodied "invisible hand"—change emerges because of the choices we make.

The movement into the knowledge age is happening because of us, not to us. Through the ways in which we change our thinking about the world, the world is changed.

If I have added one insight, shifted one viewpoint, caused one person to rethink next week's agenda, moved one business leader to reassess the next knowledge initiative's objectives—then I have accomplished my end, which was to change the world, at least to a small degree, one mind at a time.

About the Author

A self-described "business philosopher" Stowe Boyd is an expert on the strategic application of information technology. Stowe explores his varied interests, insights, and opinions in several forums: EdgeCity (edgecity.convey.com), a web site published by Stowe's consulting firm, Running Light Inc., that reviews web-based groupware; a monthly column coauthored with Jeff Angus,

"*On Knowledge Management*," published by the Lotus Developer Network; "*Update*," a quarterly supplement to "*Knowledge and Process Management*" offered by John Wiley and Sons; and frequent articles in "*KM World*" and "*KM Magazine*."

Further Reading

Bateson, Gregory. *Steps Toward an Ecology of Mind*. Northvale, NJ: 1987.

de Geus, Arie. *The Living Company*. Boston: Harvard Business School Press, 1997.

Drucker, Peter. *Post-Capitalist Society*. New York: Harper Business, 1993.

Fuller, Buckminster. *Education Automation*. Carbondale, IL: Southern Illinois University Press, 1968.

Handy, Charles. *The Age of Paradox*. Boston: Harvard Business School Press, 1995.

Handy, Charles. *The Age of Unreason*. Boston: Harvard Business School Press, 1990.

Kauffman, Stuart. *At Home in the Universe*. New York: Oxford University Press, 1995.

McLuhan, Marshall. *Understanding Media*. New York: McGraw-Hill, 1964.

Porter, Michael. *Competitive Advantage*. New York: The Free Press, 1985.

Schwartz, Peter. *The Art of the Long View*. New York: Currency Doubleday, 1996.

Senge, Peter. *The Fifth Discipline*. New York: Doubleday Currency, 1990.

Wiener, Norbert. *The Human Use of Human Beings*. Garden Cit y, NY: Doubleday Anchor Books, 1954.

www.ingramcontent.com/pod-product-compliance
Lightning Source LLC
Chambersburg PA
CBHW030859180526
45163CB00004B/1640